Firefly Friend

by Kimberly Wagner Klier
Illustrated by Michael Garland

SCHOLASTIC INC.

New York   Toronto   London   Auckland   Sydney
Mexico City   New Delhi   Hong Kong   Buenos Aires

For my mother, Mary Byrd
—K.W.K.

To Peggy
—M.G.

Reading Consultants
Linda Cornwell
Literacy Specialist

Katharine A. Kane
Education Consultant
(Retired, San Diego County Office of Education and San Diego State University)

ISBN 0-516-25235-6

12 11 10 9 8 7 6 5 4 3 2 1   5 6 7 8 9 10/0

Printed in the U.S.A   61

First Scholastic paperback printing, March 2005

Firefly friend comes out to play
when the sun is tucked away.

4

His light blinks far across the lawn.

His light blinks off.
His light blinks on.

His light blinks high
in the apple tree.

9

His light blinks off.
Where can he be?

His little light blinks a bright "hello."

His light blinks off.
Where did he go?

His light blinks on beside my ear.

What does he say? I try to hear.

Does he wish me a happy night?

He blinks at me. I think he might.

His light blinks out across the lawn.

It's time for bed. I start to yawn.

I'll sleep for now,
but tomorrow night,

I'll look again for firefly light.

Word List (63 words)

a	ear	it's	start
across	far	lawn	sun
again	firefly	light	the
apple	for	little	think
at	friend	look	time
away	go	me	to
be	happy	might	tomorrow
bed	he	my	tree
beside	hear	night	try
blinks	hello	now	tucked
bright	high	off	what
but	his	on	when
can	I	out	where
comes	I'll	play	wish
did	in	say	yawn
does	is	sleep	

About the Author

Kimberly Wagner Klier is an author and grade school teacher. She lives in Indiana with her husband Tim. They raise Appaloosa horses and two dogs, Brownie and Max.

About the Illustrator

Michael Garland lives in Patterson, New York. Besides illustrating, Michael enjoys writing and has penned many children's books and articles for *American Artist* Magazine.